# LUDWIG VAN BEETHOVEN

# Symphonies Nos. 8 and 9

## IN FULL SCORE

DOVER PUBLICATIONS, INC., NEW YORK

This Dover edition, first published in 1989, is a republication of the last
two of the *Symphonies de Beethoven. Partitions d'Orchestre,* originally
published by Henry Litolff's Verlag, Braunschweig, n.d. Lists of
instruments, a table of contents, and translations of
the vocal texts have been added.

*Library of Congress Cataloging-in-Publication Data*

Beethoven, Ludwig van, 1770–1827.
[Symphonies, no. 8, op. 93, f major] Symphonies nos. 8 and 9.

The 2nd work for solo voices (SATB), mixed chorus, and orchestra.
German text of the 2nd work by Friedrich Schiller.
Reprint. Originally published: Symphonies de Beethoven.
Braunschweig : H. Litolff's Verlag, 18—?
With English translation of the text of the 2nd work.
1. Symphonies—Scores.   2. Schiller, Friedrich, 1759–1805—Musical
settings. I. Beethoven, Ludwig van, 1770–1827. Symphonies, no. 9,
op. 125, D minor. 1989. II. Title.
M1001.B4      op. 93      1989        88-753935
ISBN-13: 978-0-486-26035-8
ISBN-10: 0-486-26035-6

Manufactured in the United States by LSC Communications
26035622    2020
www.doverpublications.com

# Contents

# Instrumentation

## SYMPHONY NO. 8

2 Flutes [Flauti, Fl.]
2 Oboes [Oboi, Ob.]
2 Clarinets (B♭) [Clarinetti, Cl.]
2 Bassoons [Fagotti, Fag.]
2 Horns (F, B♭ basso) [Corni, Cor.]
2 Trumpets (F) [Trombe, Tr.]
Timpani [Tp.]
Violins, I, II
Violas
Cellos
Basses

## SYMPHONY NO. 9

Piccolo [Flauto piccolo]
2 Flutes [Flauti, Fl.]
2 Oboes [Oboi, Ob.]
2 Clarinets (B♭, C, A) [Clarinetti, Cl.]
2 Bassoons [Fagotti, Fag.]
Contrabassoon [Contrafagotto, Ctr. Fag.]

4 Horns (D, B♭ basso, B♭, E♭)
  [Corni, Cor.]
2 Trumpets (D, B♭) [Trombe, Tr.]
Alto Trombone [Tb.]
Tenor Trombone [Tb.]
Bass Trombone [Tb. B.]
Timpani [Tp.]
Triangle [Triangolo]
Cymbals [Cinelli]
Bass Drum [Gran Tamburo]
Violins I, II
Violas
Cellos
Basses

Soprano Solo
Alto Solo
Tenor Solo
Bass-Baritone Solo

Sopranos
Altos
Tenors
Basses

# Translation of Vocal Texts in Last Movement

*(Extracts from Friedrich Schiller's "To Joy")*

*Page 176, Recitativo, words by Beethoven:*
O friends, not these tones! rather, let us begin to sing more pleasant and more joyful ones.

*Pages 178 ff.:*
Joy, beautiful divine spark, maiden from Elysium: we are intoxicated with fire, heavenly being, as we enter your sanctuary! Your spells reunite what fashion has rigidly sundered; all men become brothers wherever your gentle wing reposes.

Let whoever has gained the great stake and has become friend of a friend, let whoever has won a lovely woman, add his jubilation to ours! Yes, whoever in the world merely calls a soul his own! And let whoever has never been able to do so, steal away in tears from this company.

All beings drink joy at the breasts of nature; all good men, all evil men follow her trail of roses. She gave us kisses and the vine, a friend tested in death; sexual pleasure was granted to the worm, and the cherub stands in the sight of God!

*Pages 194 ff.:*
Happily as His suns fly through heaven's splendid field, run your course, brothers, joyfully as a hero to victory.

Joy, beautiful divine spark . . . (etc.) gentle wing reposes.

*Pages 209 ff.:*
Be embraced, O millions. This kiss for the whole world! Brothers! above the starry tent a loving Father must dwell. You fall down, O millions? Do you have a presentiment of the Creator, O world? Seek Him above the starry tent! Over stars He must dwell.

*Pages 215 ff.:*
{ Joy, beautiful divine spark . . . (etc.) sanctuary!

{ Be embraced, O millions . . . (etc.) whole world!

You fall down. . . (etc.) Father must dwell.

*Pages 231 ff.:*
Joy . . . (etc.) wing reposes.

*Pages 242 ff.:*
Be embraced . . . (etc.). Joy . . . (etc.)!

# Symphony No. 8 in F Major, Op. 93

1

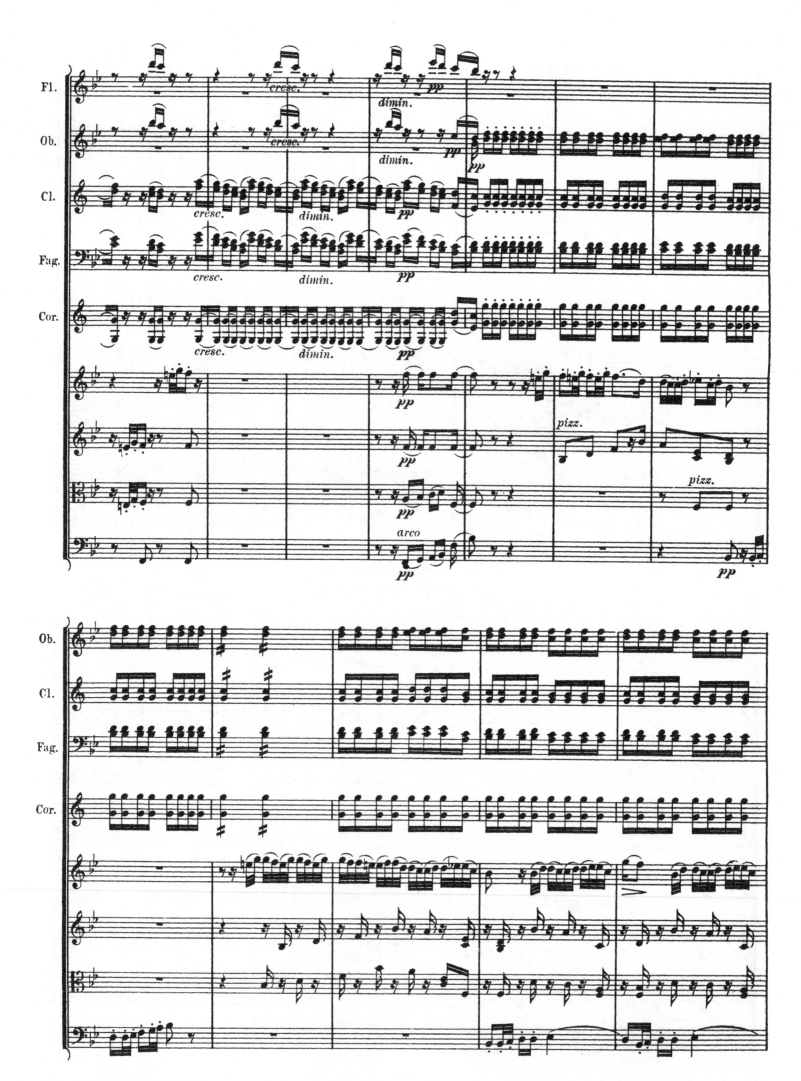

# Symphony No. 9 in D Minor, Op. 125

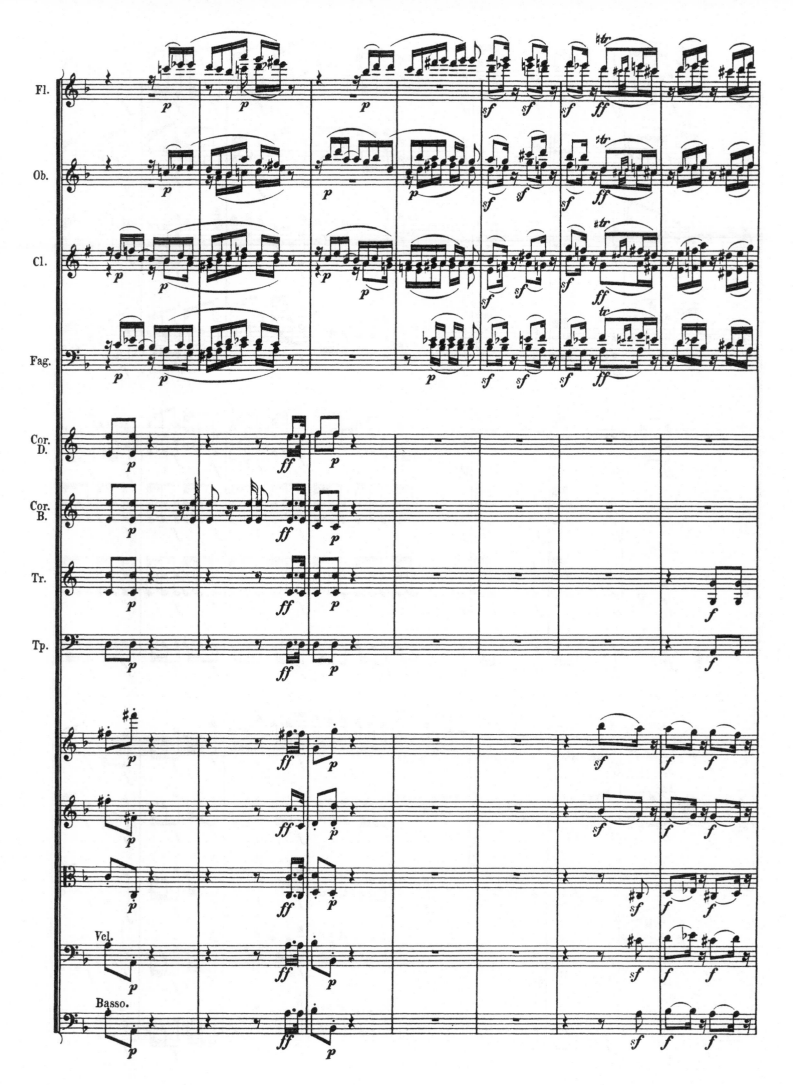

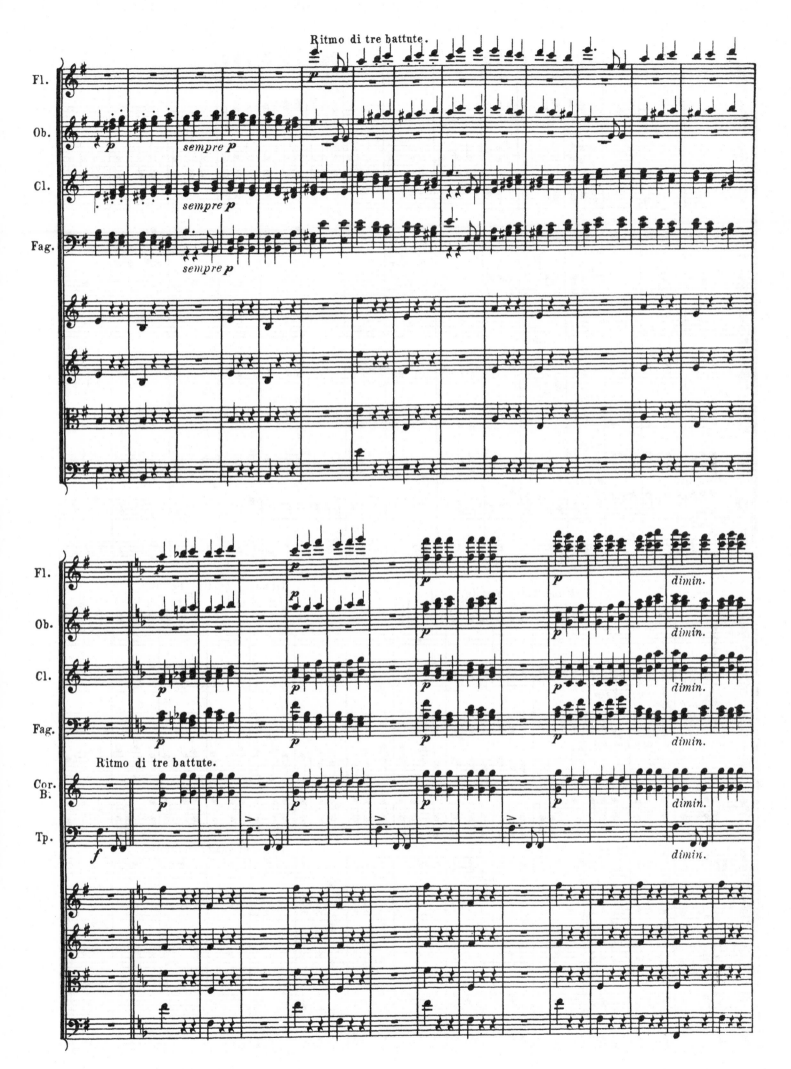

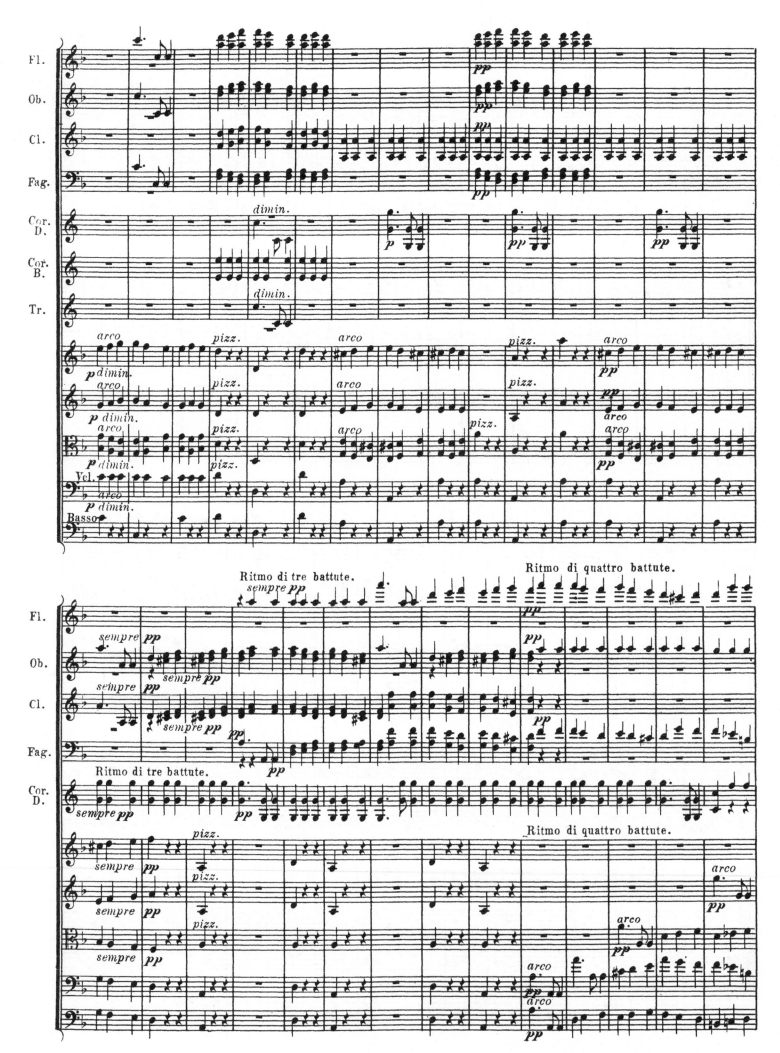

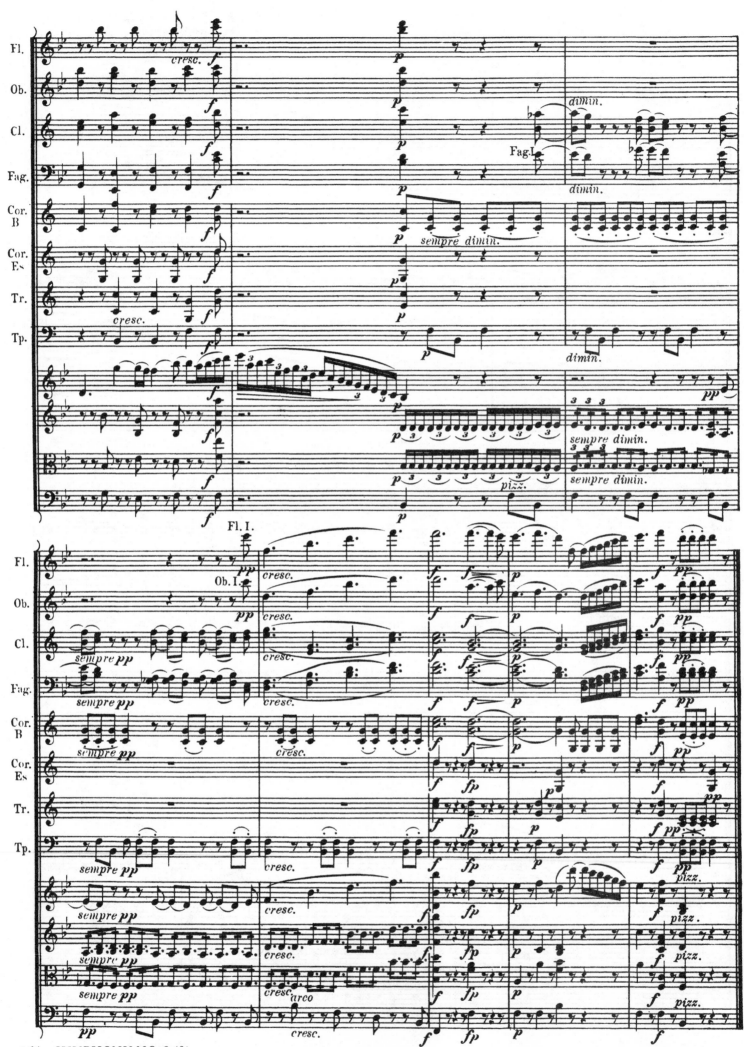

*) Selon le caractère d'un Récitatif, mais in Tempo.
In the nature of a recitative, but in tempo.

SYMPHONY NO. 9 (4)    165

nehmere an - stimmen,     und freu - - - - - - denvollere.

wir be-tre-ten feu-er-trunken,Himmlische,dein Hei-ligthum! Dei-ne Zauber bin-den wieder,was die Mode streng getheilt;al-

le Menschenwerden Brü-der, wo dein sanfter Flü-gel weilt.

Deine Zauber binden wieder, was die Mo-de streng getheilt; al -

Deine Zauber binden wieder, was die Mo-de streng getheilt; al -

Deine Zauber binden wieder, was die Mo-de streng getheilt; al -

ALLA MARCIA.
Allegro assai vivace. 𝅗𝅥. = 84.
Flauto piccolo.
Flauti.
Oboi.
Clarinetti in B.
Fagotti.
Contrafagotto.
Allegro assai vivace. 𝅗𝅥. = 84.
Corni in D.
Corni in B.
Tromba I in D.
Tromba II in B.
Timpani.
Triangolo.
Cinelli.
Gran Tamburo.
Allegro assai vivace. 𝅗𝅥. = 84.
Violino I.
Violino II.
Viola.
Tenore Solo.
CORO.
Tenore I.
Tenore II.
Bassi.
Violoncello, e Basso.
pp

froh, wie sei_ne Son_nen flie-gen durch des Himmels prächt'_gen Plan, lau_fet, Brü_der, eu_re Bahn, lau_fet,

Brü_der, eu_re Bahn,___ freu_dig, wie ein Held zum Sie_gen, wie ein Held _____ zum Sie_gen, lau_fet, Brü_der,

NB.(Diese 6 Takte können nicht vom Chor, wohl aber vom Solosänger ausgelassen werden) *

*These 6 measures may be omitted by the soloist, but not by the chorus.

wie _ der, was die Mo _ de streng ge _ theilt. Al _ le Menschen, al _ le

wie _ der, was die Mo _ de streng ge _ theilt. Al _ le Menschen, al _ le

wie _ der, was die Mo _ de streng ge _ theilt. Al _ le Menschen, al _ le

wie _ der, was die Mo _ de streng ge _ theilt. Al _ le Menschen, al _ le